GIANLUCA SPOSITO

King Kong
The Untold Story

intra

M

Mysteria Series

Cover: Davide Minghini, *King Kong at the Rimini Fair*, June 13, 1977, Davide Minghini Archives, © Biblioteca Gambalunga Rimini.

Photo credits: Academy Awards®, Barry Nolan, Davide Minghini, Paramount Pictures, Paris Match, Screen Gems/Sony Pictures Entertainment, Prospectacle/Action films, Soto Roland F. J., Studio Canal, Warner Bros., Chris Watts/Bake Visual Effects.

The images published (low-resolution or specially degraded) under Copyright Italian Law 633/1941 and the Berne Convention are predominantly simple or purely documentary photographs, over 20 years old, and serve to illustrate and validate the text, which is a work of study and divulgation. The Author and the Publisher disclaim any liability arising from different uses or misuses of them. As far as possible, the Editor has tried to trace the name of the author of all published images to notify them. The Publisher apologizes for any errors, gaps or omissions, and as of now he is willing to revise the contents in any reprints and recognize the relevant rights under the relevant regulations.

King Kong © 1933 RKO/Warner Bros.
King Kong © 1976 De Laurentiis/Paramount Pictures/Studio Canal

This book is a work of scholarship, unrelated to any trademark status and represents no venture of any of the above-mentioned companies.

Referential usage of the name King Kong and related images is not to be construed as a challenge to any trademark status. The related pictorial material that appears here is for the sole purpose of illustrating the creative processes involved in the making of the motion pictures discussed.

Index

INDEX	3
INTRODUCTION	5
THE ORIGINS OF THE MYTH	9
KONG'S CHARACTER	9
THE KONG OF 1933	15
1976, THE YEAR OF BIG KONG	25
FROM TORRE ANNUNZIATA TO KING KONG	25
BIG KONG	29
CHRISTMAS 1976: BIG KONG ON THE BIG-SCREEN	51
BIG KONG IN SOUTH AMERICA	55
LOS ANGELES TO BUENOS AIRES	55
DESTINATION: BRAZIL. BUT WITHOUT A TOOTH	73
AND AFTER BRAZIL?	79
THE OTHER KONG	83
THE KONG OF THE LAST SCENE	83
SLEEPING BEAUTY GOES TO PARIS	89
KONG IN FERRERI'S "BYE BYE MONKEY?"	95
KONG IN ROMAGNA, ITALY	101
CIRCUS PHENOMENON	109
CONCLUSIONS	111
BIBLIOGRAPHY	113
ESSAYS AND ARTICLES	113
SITES	115

Introduction

That of King Kong is one of the most classic and disturbing stories: a subject of dreamlike violence, not without a soft poetic quality, which has captivated millions of viewers and readers over the years. A superb creature in which the myth of Beauty and the Beast is revived in modern terms: an emblem of the brutal and irrepressible, yet fundamentally vital, force of nature. But also a metaphor, perhaps, for that instinctive part of the human soul, radicalized by civilization. As in Mary Wollstonecraft Shelley's *Frankenstein*, here too a monstrous being destroys and succumbs in the attempt to fulfill his desires; but if there was a creature of science, here the protagonist is the brutal and irrepressible force of nature and instincts, which civilization nevertheless seeks to dominate.

Cinematically, King Kong has experienced three milestones: in 1933, with the first film produced and directed by Merian C. Cooper and Ernest B. Schoedsack; in 1976, with the version directed by John Guillermin and produced by Dino De Laurentiis; and finally, in 2005, with the remake directed, produced, and co-written by Peter Jackson.

In 90 years of history, very different generations have thus been introduced to and thrilled by the legendary Kong. The technologies used in those three films were just as different: the technologies used by Jackson were predominantly and predictably digital (above all, the motion capture system); the others were naturally 'analog' - although the special effects and visual tricks of the 1933 edition, in fact revolutionary at the time (such as the combination of stop-motion, rear projection, matte painting and miniatures), still prove fascinating.

But in these two albeit extraordinary films from 1933 and 2005, a real giant gorilla never existed: neither trained nor mechanically animated. Perhaps viewers of the 1930s and 1940s, in their technological simplicity, might have been deluded that this was not the case by those never-before-seen effects; but certainly not those of the third millennium, well aware that digital technology was long ago capable of reproducing anything.

A separate discussion deserves, however, the 1976 film for which the producer wanted a real mechanized giant gorilla to be built: he had to be the undisputed star. Forget all other fictions, miniatures and so on: the giant gorilla had to be there. It was indeed there, it is true, but things did not turn out exactly as they thought and as we are still led to believe.

Therefore, this is the sad story of what was supposed to be an absolute giant protagonist, but whose true glory on screen was very short-lived.

To my father Domenico, who was born in 1933 when the first *King Kong* was released in theaters, a product of Merian C. Cooper's imagination, who died in 1973 when I was born.

The origins of the myth

Kong's character

The character of Kong is the brainchild of Merian C. Cooper (1893-1973), an American director, screenwriter and producer.

The screenplay for the first film (1933) was initially assigned by Cooper to Edgar Wallace, a world-renowned author of adventure and mystery novels who was already in a professional relationship with the former's film production company, the legendary RKO.

Wallace loves the initial idea Cooper developed; and the latter, taking advantage of the former's fame, would have liked to publish the novel before the film's release - which would thus have been "based on Edgar Wallace's novel," making it more appealing for the audience. Wallace was a legendarily prolific and fast writer (he could write an entire novel in a weekend...). He began writing the screenplay on January 1, 1932, and finished a first draft entitled *The Beast* on January 5.

Imaged by Heritage Auctions, HA.com

Cooper considers the draft a good start, but Wallace dies of pneumonia a month later, on February 10, 1932, just as he begins to revise the text. The script then passes into the hands of James Ashmore Creelman and Ruth Rose, who complete the work entitled Kong.

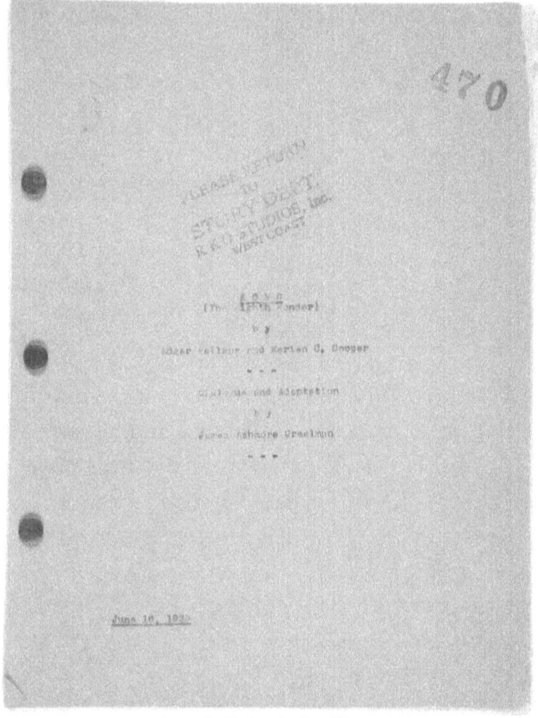

Imaged by Heritage Auctions, HA.com

The publicity campaign for the film (which will be called, by direct intervention of the producers, *King Kong*) begins in December 1932 - three months before its theatrical release - through the publication of the story as a novel.

In Cooper's intentions, the novel was to be carried out by the late Wallace, later replaced by Delos W. Lovelace.

And it is at this point that one of the many mystifications that characterize the history, cinematic and literary, of Kong begins. Mystery magazine indeed serializes the novel, while promoting it as "Edgar Wallace's last and greatest creation."

Later, other publishers (in Italy it is translated and published only in 1971) also promote the book by attributing its authorship to Wallace on the cover, rather than just the subject (along with Cooper).

But let us return to the title that Wallace himself had wanted to give to his draft screenplay (which, moreover, was extremely different from the one on which the film would later be based): *The Beast*. An explicit reference to the fairy tale of Beauty and the Beast, which, as a fairy tale, originated from Madame Leprince de Beaumont, the major eighteenth-century storyteller for children who lived in the 1700s, and quickly became a myth.

The tale is well known: it is based on the sacrifice of a very beautiful maiden who, in order to save her father from the clutches of a 'beast,' sacrifices herself; but then she slowly falls in love with the 'beast,' because she is able to see qualities hidden beneath the monster's guise and through her feeling she succeeds in redeeming him. It describes the fascination and desire that the combination of animality and primal instinct has on women; but also, according to another interpretation, the ability of a woman's love to transform a primitive and brutal feeling into something human and measured (the transformation into a Prince).

The story of Beauty and the Beast appears in many other cultures, and in various forms. There are 179 tales from different countries on a similar theme. And the cinema has tackled it several times, starting right from 1933's *King Kong*, firmly centered on a Beast who has no hope of transforming into a Prince and who becomes a symbol both of nature as opposed to civilization, and of some censored components of the human psyche, especially the male, such as the will to power and sexual desire.

The film evidently was meant to capture and satisfy the imagination of the 1933 audience, which, in the words of the historian of philosophy Francis Adorno, was "pouring with impotence" socially and economically (let's remember the 1929 crisis and the lasting consequences of those years).

Before anything else, King Kong is a monster, a *monstrum*, and in Latin the term has a double meaning: it means 'portent,' 'prodigy,' 'miracle,' as well as 'horror,' 'nefariousness,' monster precisely. Emil Cioran in *The Inconvenience of Being Born* effectively and clearly explains the fascination of monsters on a cultural, aesthetic and emotional level: 'a monster, however horrible it may be, secretly attracts us, haunts us, obsesses us, represents our privileges and miseries magnified, proclaims us, is our standard bearer.'

The monstrous inevitably attracts. The young scholar Ludovico Cantisani rightly notes: the monstrous "draws attention but also repulsion to itself, it embodies a force of nature not yet tamed, certainly anterior to every civilization and humanity itself, admirable, enviable, but at the same time, precisely because it is untamed, terribly dangerous for every social balance". So, in that historical time, with the effects of the '29 crisis still far from having disappeared, King Kong may be the perfect representation of a blind rebellion against all the social, political and economic constraints that characterize the West of those years; but, at the same time, also the demonstration of its futility, its inescapable failure. King Kong climbs the symbol of civilization and the West, that skyscraper - the Empire State Building - a wonder of the modern world, but he dies, killed by a civilization that loves being under the spotlight. A story, this one, which is renewed from film to film, with some variation, but which preserves an unchanged underlying archetypal substructure.

The Kong of 1933

But what, concretely, does the Beast from the 1933 film look like? An articulated puppet only 45 centimeters tall, with a steel skeleton covered in latex, foam rubber, and rabbit fur. Four are made: two used for the jungle scenes, one for those in the city, and another for the final sequence in which the character falls from the Empire State Building. The models - designed and built by Mexican artist Marcel Delgado based on Charles R. Knight's iconic depictions - differ slightly in the features of the snouts, the finish of the fur, and the length of the arms. These puppets are then animated in stop-motion, i.e., photographed image by image, by Willis O'Brien and his team, on models representing the jungle and the city of New York, each time in a different position that corresponds to the full range of one movement.

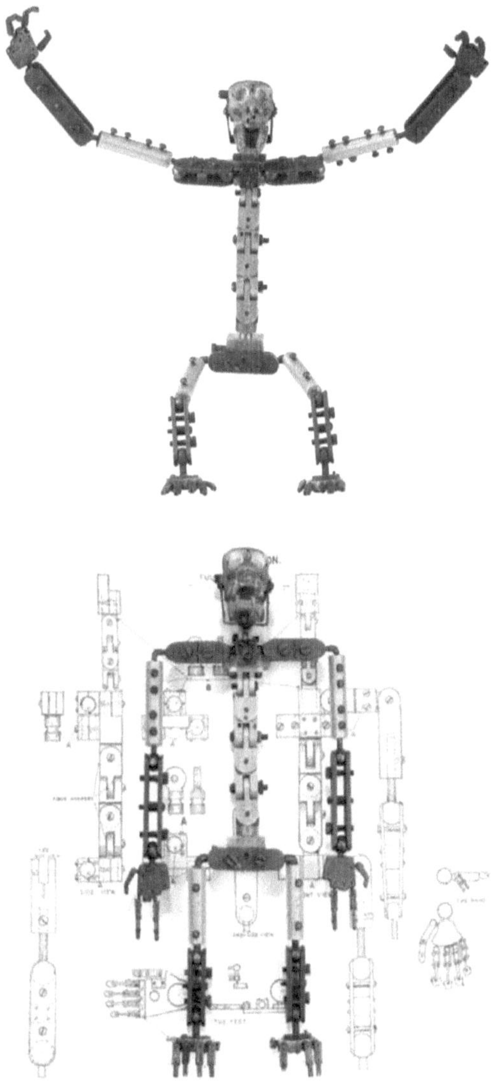

The stop-motion technique has already been in use for more than a decade, but O'Brien and other special effects technicians first used it along with other techniques, such as miniaturized projection or rear-projection, in which actors act in front of a transparent screen, behind which a previously filmed scene is projected: the two actions are filmed simultaneously so once in the film they give the idea of a single action.

So, the extraordinary and powerful Kong of 1933 is nothing more than a small puppet not even half a meter tall. Of course, some parts of him are also made 'life-size' (proportionate to a giant gorilla): for example, hand, leg and foot, and a half-bust used for some facial expressions and for some scenes in which he also uses his mouth.

While the hand and foot are largely immobile props mounted on cranes or levers to be operated, the head is a bit more complex. Made of wood and rubber and covered with bearskin, it is full of mechanisms and especially of an air compressor used to control the mouth and create facial expressions - three people are needed to operate it. The head is used for numerous close-ups and, after production, for publicity of the film. It is then placed in the forecourt of Grauman's Chinese Theatre in Hollywood for its world premiere on March 23, 1933.

Movie poster of the 1933 film

In short, as outstanding as it is and an extraordinary example of the power and magic of cinematic art, the 1933 King Kong does not star any real giant. Even the 'big bust' did not end well: ending up on the roof of Malibu's "Big Rock Beach Cafe" to attract tourists, it was slowly eroded by the salt. And it did not survive.

Forty years later, however, there are still those who believe that King Kong should be reborn, and with dimensions befitting the myth.

1976, the year of Big Kong

From Torre Annunziata to King Kong

Agostino De Laurentiis known as Dino in the early 1970s has already come a long way. Not only in the literal sense - the geographical distance that separates his birthplace, Torre Annunziata, from Hollywood - but especially the distance that separates an ordinary extra from a big star, in this case a real Hollywood tycoon. The producer, who moved to America in 1972, already had major successes behind him: from Sidney Lumet's *Serpico* (1973) to Sydney Pollack's *Three Days of the Condor* (1975), preceded by major Italian titles and even an Oscar (that for Federico Fellini's *Nights of Cabiria* as the best foreign film in 1958). In late 1974 Paramount, which distributes many of De Laurentiis' films on American soil, expressed to the producer a willingness to make a film about a 'monster,' of whatever genre. And it was the subsequent sight of a King Kong poster in his daughter's bedroom that generated an idea in his mind: to make a remake of the mythical 1933 film.

De Laurentiis loves that story, which is the story of a 'monster' but also an adventure story, a fairy tale, a comedy and, above all, a love story. After all, as he will have to say several times after the making of the film, "when Jaws [the protagonist of Spielberg's 1975 film] dies, nobody cries, but when Kong dies, everybody cries"). The story of Kong is, therefore, a universal, cross-cultural story, that appeals a vast audience - the perfect mix for a major box office success.

Thus, on May 6, 1975, the producer buys from RKO the rights to make a remake of King Kong (a court dispute with rival Universal also follows, but that is another story). The film was announced even before filming began, because on November 30, 1975, a full-page advertisement, commissioned by De Laurentiis and Paramount, appeared in the *New York Times*, featuring the image that would become the film's poster (a splendid illustration by John Berkey): Kong straddling the twin towers of the World Trade Center (built only two years earlier) with a woman in his left hand and an airplane in his right. The text of the ad reads thus, "There is still only one King Kong. One year from today, Paramount Pictures and Dino De Laurentiis will bring to you the most exciting original motion picture event of all time."

The impact is considerable, but the announcement imposes tremendous pressure on the entire production and cast, who are obliged to make within 12 months a film that, for complexity, under normal conditions would have required at least 18 months.

King Kong '76, directed by John Guillermin (who is remembered for the worldwide success of the 1974 disaster-movie *The Towering Inferno*), was certainly a much larger and more complex production than the original 1933 film, and the first filming didn't start until January 14, 1976. But it was, above all, a production characterized by De Laurentiis' wish to bring Kong to life without making use of the stop-motion technique. In short: without the puppets and miniatures of '33.

Big Kong

When pre-production on the film begins in October 1975, one of the creative team's first tasks is to figure out how to bring Kong to life. The one method that De Laurentiis does not want to use is stop-motion animation: in addition to not wanting to imitate the original film, De Laurentiis feels that stop-motion is not fluid enough and that the production is too expensive and time-consuming. After discussing the matter with the director and production team, De Laurentiis, in order to make Kong on screen, decided to use a man in a monkey costume, although much more realistic and cutting-edge than those used in the Japanese films that have since dealt with the character. Wanting a Kong capable of expressing a wide range of emotions, the creative team initially decided that rather than a mask, they would use makeup for his face. The makeup, used in the *Planet of the Apes* films, is applied directly to the actor's face, allowing him to create a full range of expressions. In the end, however, they decided to follow what Rick Baker, who will later become a true makeup wizard, suggested. Rick Baker will later be winner of 7 Oscars out of 11 nominations, and also the author, among other things, of Michael Jackson's makeup in the very famous Thriller video clip in 1983. In 1975 he was at the beginning of his own extraordinary but already brilliant career and he developed a monkey suit for the occasion.

However, since this is a gigantic creature that must interact with human performers, De Laurentiis and Guillermin feel it is important to have a life-size Kong as well. Thus, they decided to build a large Kong capable of some limited head and arm movements to be used in some shots. The team also decides to create a pair of life-size articulated hands (operated by hydraulic devices) that can be used to pick up the girl (Jessica Lange in her first role) and hold her when needed.

Producer Dino De Laurentiis and Kong's mechanical arm.

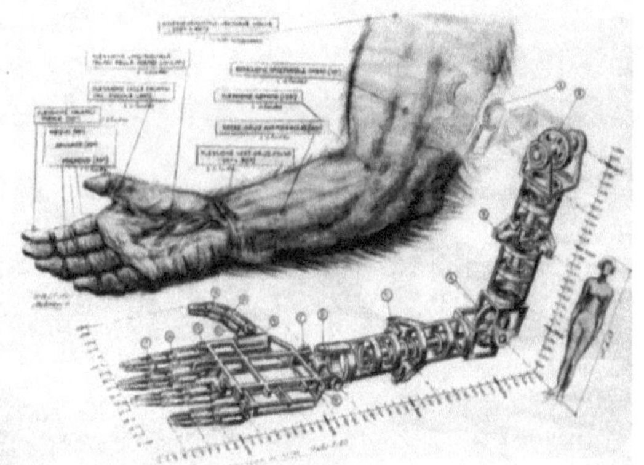

Technical drawing of the mechanical arm

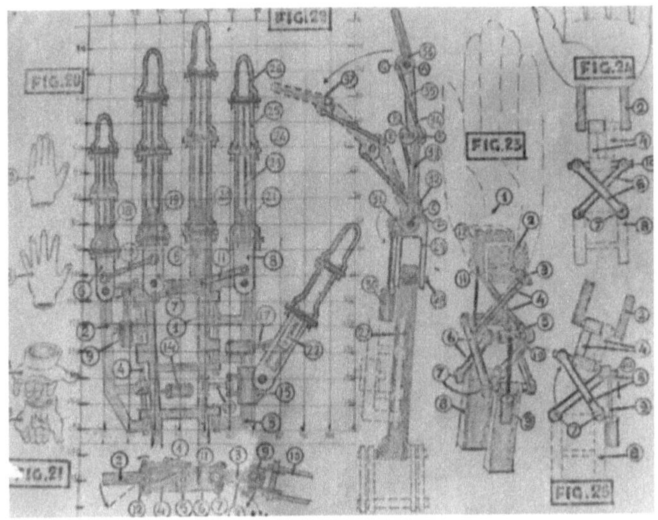

Technical drawing of the hand

To manage all special effects, De Laurentiis hired Carlo Rambaldi, who he considers already a genius (and who will win 3 Oscars for special effects in his career). A graduate of the Academy of Fine Arts in Bologna, he began frequenting film circles in Italy in 1956 when he made the sixteen-foot-long dragon Fafner for the film *Siegfried* directed by Giacomo Gentilomo, and continued by working for directors such as Mario Monicelli and Marco Ferreri, in *La Grande Bouffe*, Pier Paolo Pasolini and Dario Argento, for whom he helped create the special effects for *Deep Red* in 1975. In *King Kong* Rambaldi is primarily responsible for making some of the masks used in close-ups by Rick Baker and capable of expressing the most common emotions.

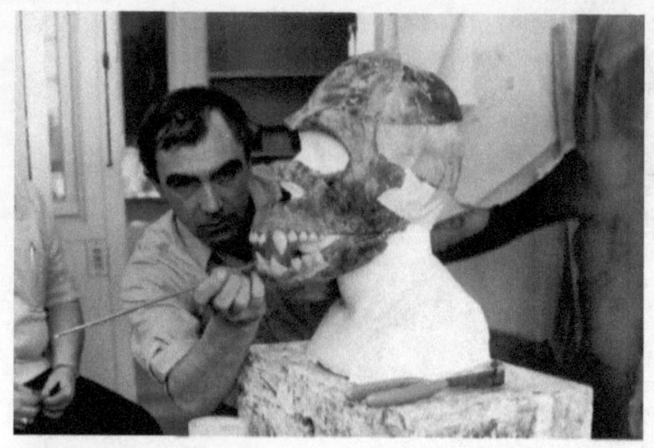

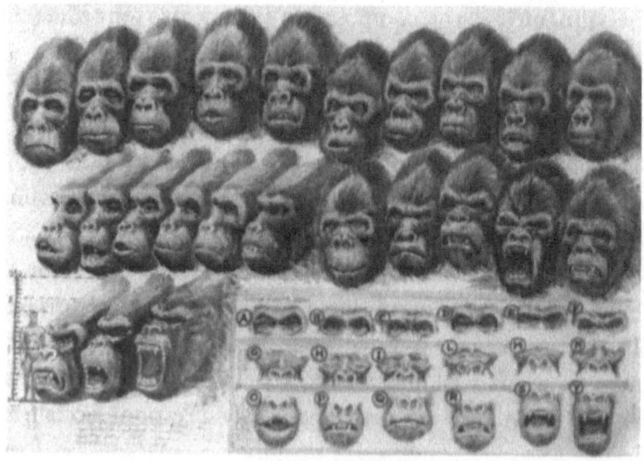

Rambaldi at work

Rick Baker with Frank Van Der Veer and Barry Nolan

But one of Rambaldi's most arduous tasks is to build the 'Big Kong.' Construction does not begin until late February

1976, increasing the size of the 'artifact' even more: to be proportionate to the giant hand capable of 'holding' the lead actress, the giant must necessarily be 42 feet, that is, over 12 meters tall. Like the armor created by Marcel Delgado forty-three years earlier, Big Kong's basic skeleton is made of aluminum. Its many joints are equipped with hydraulic cylinders, and the mechanical systems are operated by a control panel overseen by six people. The entire construction was made with cranes and supported by scaffolding. For Kong's exterior, several pieces of fiberglass are assembled, then attached to the aluminum skeleton.

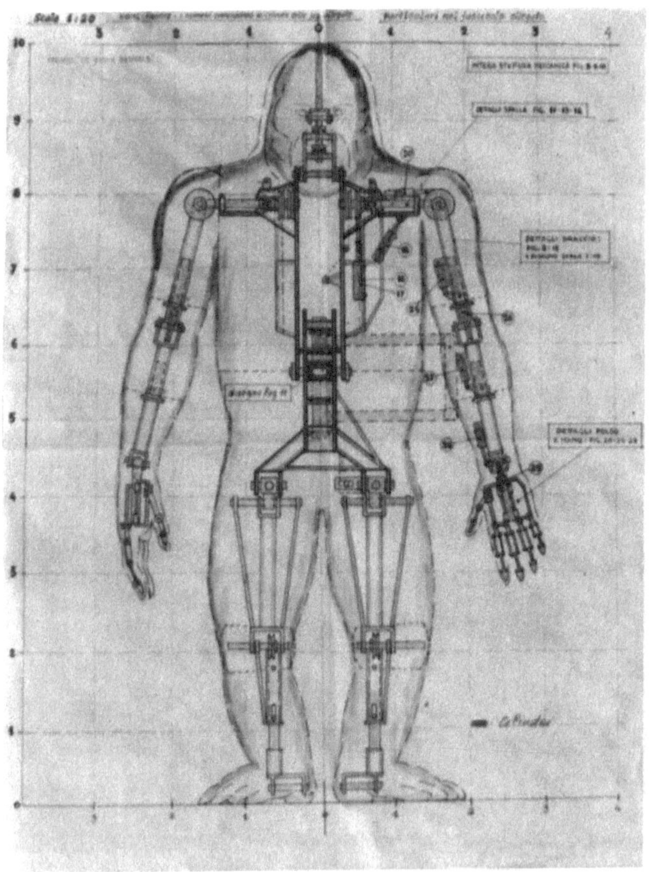

Technical drawing of the *animatronic*

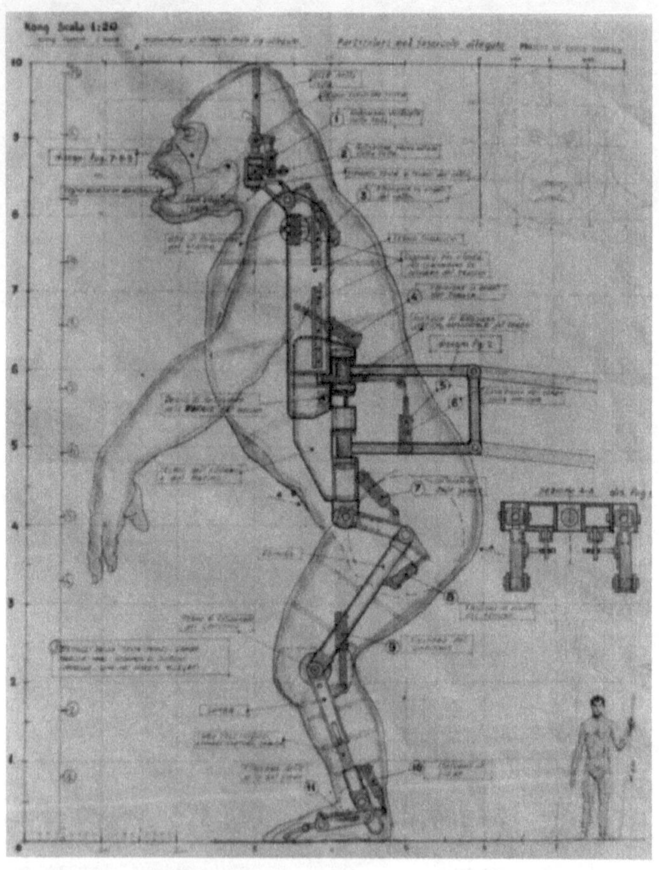

Animatronic technical drawing - Profile

Hollywood wig manufacturer Michael Dino is asked to create Kong's skin. To do so, Dino imports 4,000 pounds (1.8 tons) of horsehair from Argentina and has it dyed a uniform color. The hairs are woven into a mesh that was glued onto latex panels, then attached to Kong's fiberglass and resin exterior. The final structure weighs six and a half tons, contains 3,100 meters of hydraulic pipes and 4,500 meters of electrical cables. The robot's chest is six meters wide and both arms are six meters long. It can turn its head, raise its arms, open its mouth, flex its chest and move its fingers, eyes and toes. It took four and a half months to build at a cost of about $1.7 million.

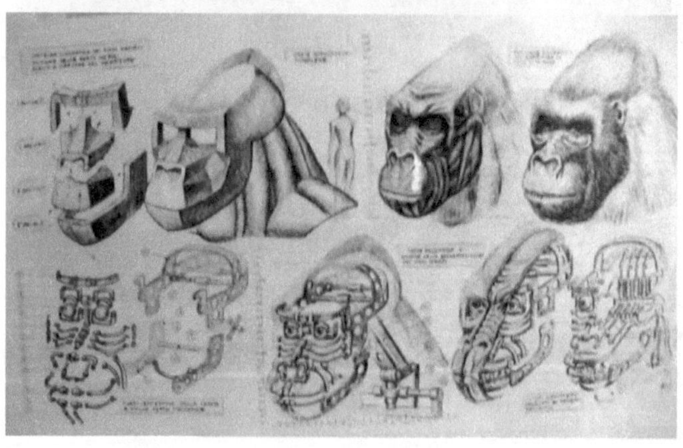

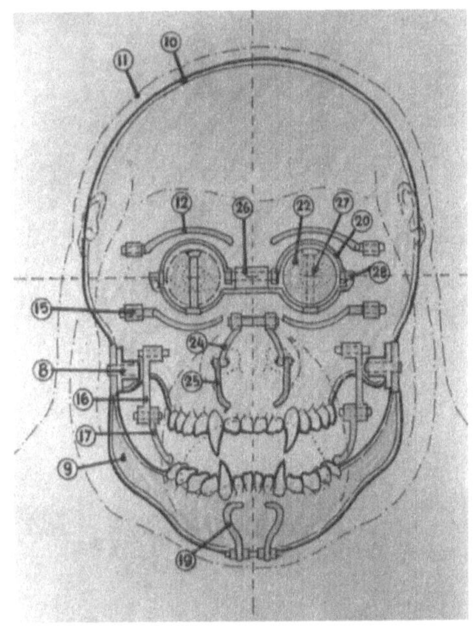

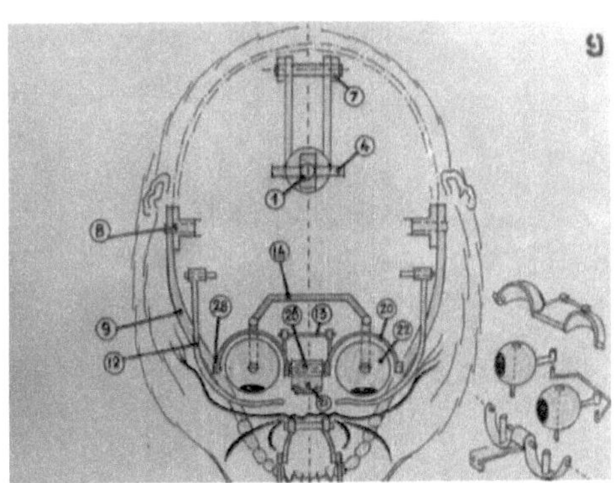

Technical drawings of Kong's head

From the moment he announced his intention to remake King Kong until its release more than a year later, Dino De Laurentiis' had only one message for the audience: they would see a 40-foot-tall robot Kong.

Carlo Rambaldi on the set of the film (1976)

Jessica Lange on the set of the film (1976)

De Laurentiis knows that an expensive, innovative new Kong film cannot use a "man in an ape suit." Or, at the very least, people must not know about it... And in fact, the first preventive measure taken by the production is to keep quiet the role of Rick Baker and his suit - even though it represented a revolutionary technology that ushered in a new era of animatronic special effects.

Dino De Laurentiis on the set of the film (1976)

De Laurentiis' ultimate goal is to convince the audience that they are really watching a 40-foot gorilla on the screen. Of course, this goal is impossible to achieve: the audience knows that there is no such thing as a 40-foot gorilla. But De Laurentiis realizes that something else is possible instead: convincing the audience that they are seeing not a 40-foot gorilla, but a 40-foot robot gorilla. All he has to do is just lie.

Reading the reviews published at the time, it seems clear that critics really think that the 40-foot robot was used for a substantial part of the film. Instead, the reality is quite different from the very beginning. Indeed the extraordinary animatronic designed by Rambaldi cannot - due to the complexity and impossibility of achieving what the mask worn by Baker can do instead - be used for the majority of the film. Also, because it is not completed until June 1976.

However, De Laurentiis knows that the giant robot cannot be promoted as the absolute star of a groundbreaking film and not appear in the film. An appearance, albeit brief, must be there. This is necessary so it cannot be said that he lied; but perhaps that he exaggerated... What better then to film publicly a scene with the Big Kong and invite journalists?

Thus, from August 11 to August 20, 1976, the last major sequence of the production is filmed at the Paramount studios in Los Angeles: the scene of Kong's presentation, the one at Shea Stadium - the one in which Kong, after a long journey, is finally presented chained, briefly..., to the general public. Rambaldi's Big Kong is ready, and this is the opportunity to show the world (especially journalists) that he was not lying: the giant robot really exists. This leads, then, to certain somewhat credulous reviews, generalizing (naively at least) about the robot's use in the rest of the film.

Let's be clear: De Laurentiis was certainly not the first to 'go overboard' in presenting a film product by crafting a narrative to accompany and properly support the hyperbole of the film's giant robot protagonist. Even George Lucas, a few months later for *Star Wars* (1977), would imply that C-3PO (the android played by Anthony Daniels) and R2-D2 (the small robot played by Kenny Baker) were real robots. A documentary on the making of *Star Wars* would even describe how the robots kept breaking down during the film's production, showing C-3PO stumbling through the desert. In short, spectacle within spectacle.

The Shea Stadium scene dictates the transport in Lot 2 Paramount of the Big Kong, conveniently disassembled into pieces and then rebuilt on a large trolley designed to move on a long track in the center of the arena.

In order to have a large number of extras in the audience to fill the bleachers, the paid and planned extras are not enough. So (to save money but still have a large number of people in the bleachers) they prefer to expand it to the general public by placing an ad in the Los Angeles Times and inviting people to attend Kong's debut. The ad contains a coupon that can be used to purchase tickets - all of which sold out within a few days. On the first night about 3,000 people show up to witness the scene in which Dwan and Fred arrive in the park by helicopter. Although Big Kong is not used that night, the producers know the audience wants to see it; so when filming is complete, the lights are shined on the wall and the giant gates are opened to reveal the giant robot. Unfortunately, Kong's eyes appear crossed and a metal neck support has snapped, causing Kong's head to recline on his chest. Therefore, De Laurentiis immediately ordered to turn off the spotlights and close the gates. On the second night, the outside public is not invited and the production uses duly paid extras to film scenes of the panicked crowd running out of the park, pushing Jack and Dwan in an attempt to escape. On the third night, the general public returns, and it is the night of Big Kong's presentation. Kong was in an aluminum cage with a giant crown on his head.

The sheet used to cover him is hooked to a helicopter and lifted while four cameras film. On the first attempt, the sheet gets caught; but on the second attempt it lifts up and reveals Big Kong fully functional: his eyes roll and his fingers and toes wiggle; all while he lifts his head and opens his mouth to roar. Kong looks magnificent and the crowd cheers. It is a wonderful moment that does not last long, however, because at the end of the first shot one of Kong's hydraulic lines has a leak. John Guillermin is the first to notice it, shouting to stop the filming in obvious frustration.

The next evening, the giant robot is used again for the shot of the scene in which Kong shatters his cage. Unfortunately, the aluminum pieces are too heavy and put a strain on the hydraulic systems: the arm breaks and the jaw comes loose.

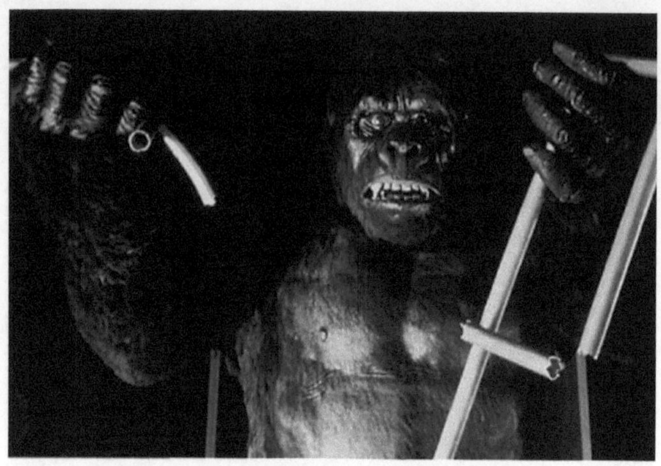

A few minutes later, he is moved from the platform and placed in the center of the arena for a shot of the crowd rushing in front of Kong as he raises his arms.

On the last night of work, Kong's right leg is detached from his body and mounted on a crane for the filming of the scene in which Kong steps on Fred Wilson (played by Charles Grodin).

In the end, Big Kong turns out to be a partial disappointment. The main problem is that he is unable to move quickly or fluidly enough to appear realistic. Thus, the mechanical monster is present in only six shots in the finished film: less than 25 seconds. While in the first few, those in which Kong is revealed, he looks really impressive, in the others he is static and unimpressive. To make matters worse there is one more aspect: he does not match Rick Baker (in the ape suit) in either appearance or movements, making the substitution painfully obvious.

Christmas 1976: Big Kong on the Big-Screen

King Kong was released in 1,200 theaters in the United States and another 1,000 theaters worldwide on Friday, December 17, 1976. At the time, it was the largest simultaneous release in film history. Accompanied by a massive promotional and merchandising campaign, a film inspired by a pop culture phenomenon was turned into one of the big events of the 1970s.

The critics welcomed the film mostly positively, and the reviews ranged from respectful to enthusiastic. *King Kong* is also a success at the box office: by March 1977 it had already earned $88 million. In the end, it grossed just over $90 million, an incredible figure for the time (just as incredible is, for the time, the amount spent on promoting the film alone, about $10 million). Not only that: there will also be television rights to top up the pot. The film would make its television debut in 1978 on NBC, which would pay De Laurentiis a whopping $19.5 million for the rights to two broadcasts over five years - at the time, the highest amount ever paid by a television network to broadcast a film.

Promotional poster for the release of the film (1976)

Two Oscar nominations: Best Cinematography and Best Sound Recording. Carlo Rambaldi, Glen Robinson and Frank Van Der Veer are also awarded a special Oscar for Best Visual Effects.

Center Carlo Rambaldi at the Oscar ceremony in 1977

Although the film was well received on its first release, its reputation has suffered greatly over the years, mainly because of those who never stopped loving the 1933 film exclusively. Still, the 1976 remake has many merits, great technological innovations ("it is an encyclopedia of special effects," as Rambaldi would call it), and treats the character of Kong with extreme affection and respect.

Of course, a few months later *Star Wars* would be released, and the film with the giant ape would seem to belong to a bygone era. Yet, to that era (and beyond) belong the many who, in the years since, have always loved that giant, and wondered: did they really use a giant robot to make the film? Then again: and where did the giant robot end up after the filming?

Big Kong in South America

Los Angeles to Buenos Aires

What happens to the mechanical Big Kong, used in the film for less than 25 seconds? For years, many have wondered; and his presence in South America in the late 1970s, led to the spread of a news story that still circulates not only among fans but also among journalists: those 12 meters of aluminum giant would end up rotting in a wasteland on the outskirts of Mar del Plata, Argentina, at the end of a failed tour. A victim of "South American primitivism," this is the recurring allusion.

An inglorious and horrible end for the already unfortunate (only theoretical) protagonist of a film that had nevertheless brought home many millions of dollars. Yet, the story of King Kong's passage through South America - between September 1978 and the end of April 1979 - is full of errors, rumors, misunderstandings, omissions and lies, dragged on and repeated to this day.

What is certain is that, immediately after the film's release, Big Kong is still of interest: it doesn't matter that he was an underutilized actor - after all, no one knows or suspects that. Kong is of interest because he is that giant robot that De Laurentiis wanted at all costs to make, and who partly determined the success of a film of which he was hardly a part. In at least one interview Baker will say he is convinced that the only reason De Laurentiis would make the film is so he could say he built the only life-size Kong ever existed...

Well, De Laurentiis has not been wrong, even regarding subsequent marketing. The interest in being able to have and display that animatronic is very strong. The first solicitation came from an Argentine businesswoman, Beky Simone Pérez Pichón, architect of the project that will bring Kong to South America and remain in the memory and imagination of thousands of Argentines for decades. Thanks to New York tycoon Larry Leeds she manages to set up a meeting in Los Angeles with Dino De Laurentiis, initiating negotiations that last a week. At the end, she ends up with $500,000 down and a contract to move and use King Kong for six months (renewable). The contract stipulates that Big Kong not move from the pelvis down (the few movements filmed were enough to make it clear to everyone not to risk any more) and that he be 'accompanied' on the tour by engineer Eddie Surkin (Kong Mechanical Coordinator)-"I won't give you Kong if you don't go with the engineer," De Laurentiis says to her.

At that point, with the contract signed, Beky Simone Pérez Pichón was able to be joined by another entrepreneur, Ricardo Gangeme, making a further agreement that included the covering (by the latter) of the sum demanded by De Laurentiis and the fair division of the subsequent revenues.

But where to take and what to make that rather static giant do? The tour is already set: first Buenos Aires, Palermo neighborhood, and then Mar de la Plata.

Meanwhile, newspapers spread the news and enthusiasm skyrockets. There are a lot of exaggerations: technological prodigy, masterpiece of cybernetics, phenomenon of technology, electronic marvel of uncanny precision. Here is how the huge gorilla is presented upon his arrival in Argentina: "(...) You will marvel at the naturalness (...)," writes *La Nación* on August 21, 1978. "He can blink, open his mouth, gesticulate and move his ears. Moreover, in action scenes, his nostrils dilate," illustrating these words with a photograph that actually shows the mask worn by Baker in the film...

On Thursday, September 7, 1978, as Argentina is enduring one of the most dramatic dictatorships of the 20th century, the famous Big Kong arrives from the United States, after a stop in Montevideo, at Pier C of the port of Buenos Aires. It arrives there sectioned and stored in 18 crates on board from the ELMA (Empresa Líneas Marítimas Argentinas) ship Jujuy II, and remains in its hold for two more days while preparations are completed for its transfer to the premises of the Sociedad Rural Argentina (SRA) in the Palermo neighborhood, as planned by the business group responsible for the entire transfer.

ELMA's JuJuy II cargo ship.

In truth, the entrepreneur, since she would not want to disassemble Kong in order to move it, even asks NASA they could do it or at least give her indications on how to do so. Having perhaps seen the movements of the rockets used for the Apollo missions (man went to the moon only a handful of years before), the same transportation technique can be adopted for Big Kong, she thinks. But not so: NASA dryly replies that the latter is a bigger and more demanding load than a lunar rocket....

Thus, it 'falls back' to the ship and a journey that lasts a month and a half. On September 9, 1978, going up Avenida Santa Fe, the boxes containing the different parts of the animatronic passed through downtown Buenos Aires in front of the astonished gazes of passersby and accompanied by Pinky, a then-famous television presenter and animator.

A very unique caravan, organized by the Román Transportation Company and filmed live by the country's leading media.

Promotional image of the Román company contracted to transport
Kong from Quay C of the Port of Buenos Aires to the premises of
the Sociedad Rural Argentina (in the Palermo neighborhood).

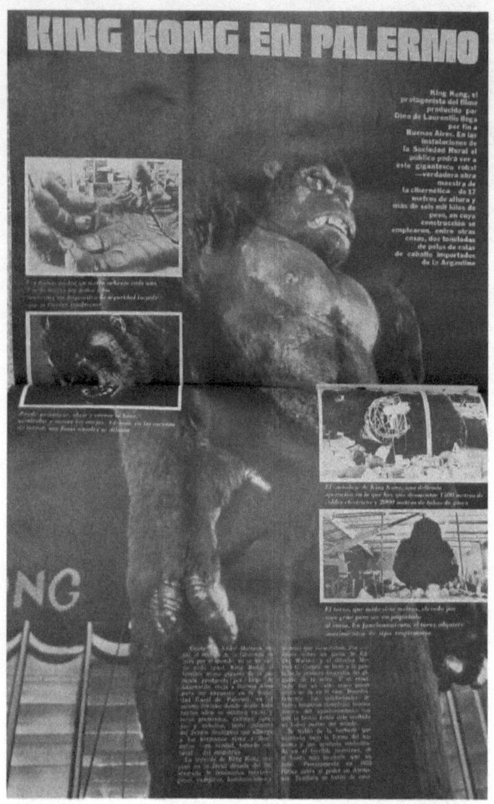

All of Avenida Santa Fe up to the Rural is packed with people. Not even for the Pope, they say, had there been such a turnout.

King Kong is in Argentina, but it takes several weeks to set up the exhibition. Also because, when everything is almost ready for the opening, a tornado takes away the marquee and ... Kong's head. Which is found not far away, but hairless. Eddie Surkin works on it day and night to make up for the delay.

At last, on September 23, 1978, the aristocratic neighborhood space opened its doors to display a mechanical marvel never before seen in these latitudes. It is arranged in a giant tent, painted blue and white, 100 long, 40 wide and 20 meters high.

The entrance to the show is located on Avenida Sarmiento (right across from the Zoo), and as soon as you enter you will find yourself in a series of very exotic huts (evoking some of the film's settings), where Kong merchandise is sold:

One of the few merchandising specimens of the time

However, since Kong, by himself, can do truly little (his legs cannot move), a larger and more engaging show is built around him.

The show is originally organized as a real play, entitled "El Paraíso de King Kong" (King Kong's Paradise). The plot takes place on an unknown island where a series of dancers are in adoration of the gorilla, while an evil Professor Neurus mistreats him to the point of anger...

Advertisement of the time

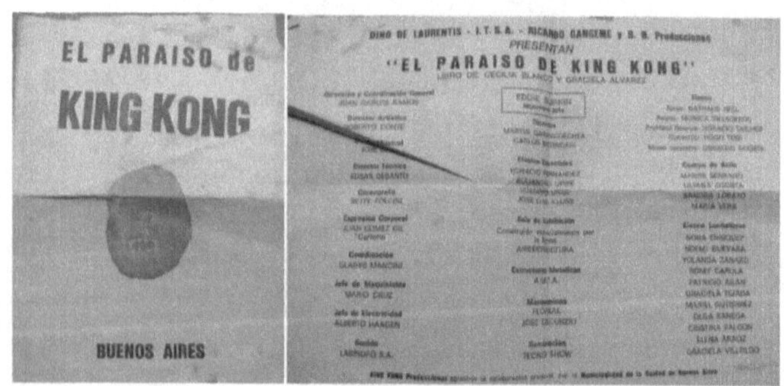

Opening program, Saturday, September 23, 1978

But the structure of the show is short-lived: people become impatient to see the giant gorilla. So, it is decided to cut the dance troupe, leaving only a few visual effects (a volcano that seems to erupt and lasers aimed at the giant). Big Kong is announced by the presence of a fake explorer with a whip in his hand. Then the curtain opens and Kong finally appears: chains on his hands, moving his face and groaning, in the midst of a mock fog and the deafening screams of the crowd.

A few days later, a real circus was added near the facility, there were also jugglers, clowns, knife throwers and some trapeze artists.

In January 1979 it is decided to move Kong from Buenos Aires to Mar de la Plata to take advantage of the summer (there, indeed, it is summer in January). Apparently, the Román Company (the same one that had brought him from the port of Buenos Aires to La Rural) is contracted to transport him to the coast with three special trucks. The site chosen to erect the marquee in which the gorilla would delight children and adults is the grounds of the former Bristol Stadium: an old boxing palace, now demolished (much to the dismay of the city's nostalgic people).

But Big Kong is so large that some special work is needed to accommodate it: the former stadium has to be modified with excavations and retaining walls to gain the height needed to accommodate Kong in a standing position, thus ending up as a kind of amphitheater. Because of the work that needed to be done, the entire month of January, the busiest month for tourists, is lost with the work.

Kong in the area of the former Bristol Stadium in Mar de la Plata.

Kong, "the greatest artist of the summer," the "technical marvel" of Dino de Laurentiis, thus tries to be part of the coastal art scene.

The Mar de la Plata show, compared to the one in Buenos Aires, is accompanied by circus artists and music acts that made it last more than half an hour and with an admission cost even double that of the capital. The debut took place on February 1, 1979.

Kong's part, limited in his ability to move, is largely determined by the audience's (mostly children's) questions and his reactions (faces), which the operators oversee accordingly always guided by Surkin. Some of the questions asked give Kong the opportunity to be euphoric ("are you happy in Argentina?"), others cause nostalgia ("do you miss your mother?"), enhance his male ego ("do you like blond girls?"), provoke astonishment ("do you use deodorant?") or provoke anger ("when you get married, will you move in with your mother-in-law?"). Each question is matched by a facial movement, manifesting different moods. Then, after an alleged outburst, he raises his arms and breaks the chains that hold him back, and, as a final scene, a blond trapeze artist hanging from a rope is placed on his right arm and lifted effortlessly.

Surkin oversees Kong's movements, teaching some of the guys in the workshop in charge of the show how to move the animatronic: one oversees the arms, another the face, and then yet another oversees the sounds at a microphone. Kong's face looks very expressive, but the rest of his body is rather static, and tied to a pole (as, incidentally, was also planned for the film production). Eddie Surkin in a brief interview with the newspaper *La Capital* on February 9, 1979 thus explains some technical details about the way Big Kong is controlled: "A control panel that is surprisingly small for the functions it has to perform, interpolates electrical or hydraulic energies to make possible the movements of King Kong, who has the ability to play each of his parts indistinctly (...). As for his voice, these are not programmed sounds but acoustic deformations of the exclamations of different people, which are emitted through microphones, with the intensity corresponding to the monkey's moods: anger, good humor, nostalgia, indifference."

However, the performance of the "eighth wonder of the world" continues to be considered rather banal and mediocre, and moreover now too expensive. In addition, many vacationers in the city have already seen him 'perform' at the Rural Buenos Aires.

The commercial failure is followed by several legal disputes due to the illegal use of music during the show and the fact that the rented tent was not paid for. In fact, the company that owns the tent ends up taking it back, leaving Big Kong even more exposed to deterioration due to the frigid autumn weather (when it's spring at our place) of the Atlantic beach.

King Kong, que Debería Hallarse Asombrando a Río, Sigue Aún Cubierto con una Lona Abandonado en Mar del Plata

El círculo muestra la gigantesca estructura de King Kong que, con sus 17 metros de altura y cuando debería estar asombrando al público de Río de Janeiro, permanece prácticamente abandonada en el centro de la ciudad de M. del Plata

MAR DEL PLATA (De nuestra agencia) — En la primavera fue el acontecimiento que movió a millares de porteños a verlo. Mucho antes, en los Estados Unidos, su monumental figura había causado el asombro de millones de espectadores. El verano último llegó a Mar del Plata y ante la expectativa general, King Kong —a él nos referimos— mostró su imponente figura en el predio de avenida Luro al 3400, más exactamente donde años atrás la Perla del Atlántico tuvo el histórico estadio Bristol. Allí la mole de diecisiete metros de altura, que realizaba movimientos y rugía al punto de hacer temblar los edificios vecinos, convocó a miles de marplatenses y turistas para brindar un espectáculo que, en ocasiones, impresionaba demasiado. Tanto que era común, cuando el cinematográfico gorila destruía paredes de utilería en una mezcla de locura y enfurecimiento, ver a madres con sus pequeños en brazos correr casi con pánico en dirección a la calle. Al fin, efecto logrado de un espectáculo que dio mucho qué hablar, pero que no se nutrió, precisamente, de críticas halagüeñas. Hoy, a más de un mes del epílogo del ciclo estival, King Kong permanece solitario, abandonado, como un gigantesco desecho más de los tantos que hay en la manzana de Luro, Jujuy, 25 de Mayo y España. Apenas cubierta su cabeza por una lona, el enorme mono se muestra erguido, tieso, con su vista puesta en la tierra. Una gran mole de diecisiete metros de altura que ahora no concita más atención que la de un simple objeto. Algo que se ve al pasar y que de inmediato, tras un ligero pensamiento, se esfuma. Ya King Kong, prácticamente sin "vida", no interesa. ¿Pero por qué su abandono? A esta altura del año, conforme los anticipos oportunos, el gran gorila debería estar rugiendo y asombrando en Río de Janeiro. Sin embargo, está acá; sin nadie que otorgue una respuesta por él. Sin embargo, abundan los comentarios, las conjeturas y las versiones en torno a su suerte. La más insistente habla de un embargo de SADAIC. Otras dicen que los reclamos financieros provienen, también, de otros sectores. Lo cierto es que King Kong continúa en Mar del Plata, a la intemperie, soportando el rigor de un otoño que pareciera ser invierno.

Kong thus remains naked and out in the open, on the grounds of the former Bristol Stadium at Avenida Luro 3400 (between Jujuy and España), barely covered by a miserable tarp.

Article in the newspaper *La Capital*, April 28, 1979

Meanwhile, Big Kong is even seized and auctioned off because of debts accrued during the show's organization. The auction is set for April 29, 1979, but on April 26, the local court suspends it: finally International Transax S.A.,

owner of the rights to use the animatronic in South America, shows up, and - due to a failed notification - appears not to have heard about the auction. It nevertheless arranges to deposit a sum sufficient to stop the proceedings, and to announce a spectacular new trip abroad.

Despite this, the state of abandonment, the passing of time, and the sudden 'disappearance' of Big Kong (in reality on his way to Brazil) caused rumors that have even reached the present day and turned into real fake news. For example, some stories place him in the abandoned area of the "Ciudad Deportiva de la Boca"; others narrate that he was bought by a sleazy circus and toured the country. It is also said that Kong would deteriorate in the "Ciudad de los Niños," near La Plata, or that he would lie, inert and disassembled, in a warehouse in the Villa Devoto neighborhood of the federal capital.

But of all these stories, for which, moreover, no firm evidence has ever existed, there is one that has ended up becoming a kind of "official narrative," the favorite perhaps because it is considered the least irrational and the most convincing. It tells that Big Kong allegedly ended up being eaten by rats and scrapped by the inhabitants of a village near the penitentiary in the town of Batán, a few kilometers from Mar del Plata, after being abandoned there.

Stories, however, have circulated to the present day, feeding the legend concerning the tragic (?) fate of the iconic monster in South America. Therefore, Kong's victim status was amplified. As if it was not enough getting riddled with bullet holes at the foot of the Twin Towers in the last scene of the film. A victim, after all, of the consumerism and opportunism of the many who have been able to exploit, if not his gifts, at least his name.

The fact is that, in May 1979, Big Kong disappears, and almost no one knows for sure where he ends up. In fact, there is a new agreement with Marcelo Gutglas, owner of the "Playcenter" amusement park in São Paulo, Brazil, who, moreover, had already come in contact in the previous months with Beky Simone Pérez Pichón expressing his interest in a subsequent transfer of the animatronic from Argentina to Brazil. This is exactly what happens.

Destination: Brazil. But without a tooth

Three trucks are allocated for special transport: on one is loaded the body with head and legs, on the other two the arms and other equipment.

They pick Kong up on Avenida Luro e España thanks to a crane, and the operation lasts until eleven o'clock in the evening. Then, however, the unexpected happens: an outbreak of fire affects the audio equipment on one of the trucks with one of Kong's arm nearby. The immediate intervention of the transport workers prevents the flames from spreading to the Kong parts and the fire is fortunately immediately circumscribed.

The next day, escorted by Traffic Police guards, the three trucks arrive in Buenos Aires and are parked in a warehouse in Calle Pareja, between Campana and Cuenca, in the Devoto neighborhood. Kong stays there for a few days because a special document for importing the cargo is needed from the Brazilian Ministry of Economy. In addition, permits from the Department of National Roads are also needed: the gorilla takes up quite a lot of roadway space, including height (4 meters, in addition to 1.5 of the trailer). It takes 20 days to start the journey again.

The itinerary includes Villa Devoto, through Route 8 to the town of Pergamino, and from there, after circling around Santa Fe, to Paso de los Libres to get to Brazil.

Of course there are problems: such as the four days it takes to manage to get under a bridge (by buying twelve super low-profile tires...).

Kong travels with his head in the open air; only the rest

of his body and, in particular, the hydraulic mechanisms are protected by tarps.

The convoy is held for four days at the border for customs formalities; then, via Route 290, it leaves for Porto Alegre, where it remains for a full week. Then, it sets off again on Route 116 toward São Paulo. Finally, Kong arrives.

King Kong enters São Paulo (Brazil)

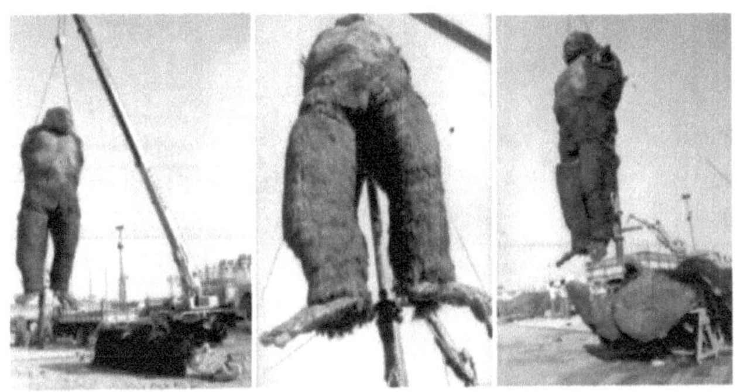

When it comes time to pick up the shipment, Playcenter owner Marcelo Gutglas has Kong inspected. And he finds a problem: some teeth were missing - what happened?

It is reconstructed, after years, studies and interviews, by an Argentine historian and university lecturer, Fernando Jorge Soto Roland (to whom we also owe the retrieval of the photos above). During Kong's stay in the warehouse on Pareja Street in the Devoto neighborhood (exactly at Calle Pareja corner Cuenca, 3200 Pareja) a group of kids - only 10 years old at the time - come across the 'monster,' lying on trucks in an open, unattended structure. They decide to do what, years later, they call a 'prank': they climb onto the iron structures of the defenseless animatronic, 'enter' it and mutilate it, removing some of its teeth, which they then distribute among their companions as loot.

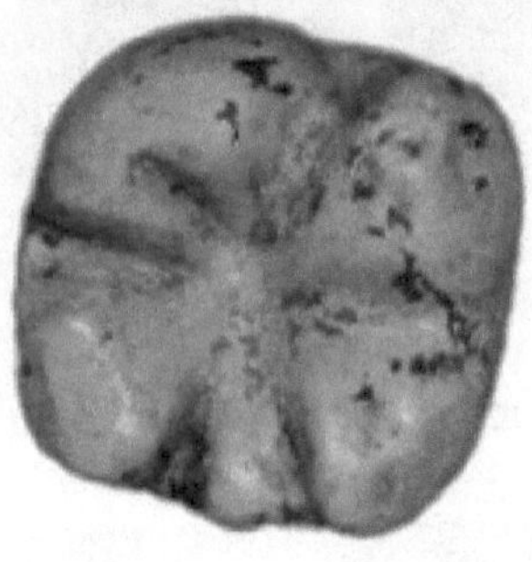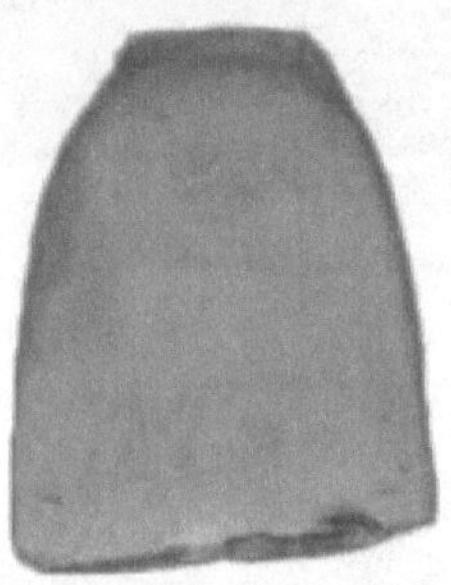

Paradoxically, it is precisely because of "Kong's teeth" that we can trace Big Kong's travel from Argentina to Brazil, disproving all the rumors that saw him abandoned and torn apart by rats in a dump in Villa Devoto. Kong only passes through Villa Devoto, and although he loses a few teeth… he then resumes his journey around the world, and even with some success in Brazil.

In fact, in an interview in 2012, Playcenter owner Marcelo Gutglas explains that King Kong's relationship with the Brazilian facility sees two key moments. The first is in 1977, when actress Jessica Lange and special effects creator Carlo Rambaldi arrive in Brazil to promote the film's release and visit the amusement park for the film's premiere. At the time, the park designs and builds a giant Kong, which is completely inanimate and non-mechanical. Subsequently, Gutglas manages to make arrangements with the organizers of the Argentine tour and secure the arrival of the real Big Kong in the park. Just the spread of the news generates mile-long lines to the facility and a record attendance, for the time, with 450,000 visitors in July 1979.

Finally, Kong receives a well-deserved success.

And after Brazil?

After his stay in Brazil, Kong continued to travel, although there is no definite information. Eddie Surkin, the engineer who controls his screams and movements through a control panel, appears to have been in charge of accompanying him everywhere, at least until 1985. But, to date, the animatronic' s individual transfers prove difficult to track down. In 1985, it appears that his travels stopped. In fact, an article that came out on Monday, April 29, 1985, in the *Times News* of Hendersonville, North Carolina (U.S.), announces that Hollywood's most famous ape is about to arrive at his final resting place. And this also is confirmed by Ray Morton, author of *King Kong: The History of Movie Icon from Fay Wray to Peter Jackson* (2005). Prompted by Fernando Jorge Soto Roland, Morton confirms what Soto Roland himself had moreover already learned through other sources: that Big Kong ended his international tours in the early 1980s, ending up in a Los Angeles warehouse near the airport.

Then, when De Laurentiis moved to North Carolina in the early 1980s, founding the De Laurentiis Entertainment Group (D.E.G.) and building the structure of what would become Carolco Studios, he welcomed Big Kong and other props to the new warehouses, partly on the assumption that he would be able to use it for the additional 1986 remake (*King Kong Lives*). In the meantime, Big Kong would undergo a major decay of the exterior structure, so deteriorated as to show the metal interior. The very condition of the mechanical giant prevented even limited use in the new 1986 film production. The movie was a box-office bomb (*King Kong Lives* grossed half of what it cost), and with others failures, led to the bankruptcy of the "De Laurentiis Entertainment Group" (D.E.G.) as early as 1988. However, some witnesses say that they saw Kong's head and one of the arms outside those Studios in those years and even afterwards. One testimony is offered by Chris Watts (visual effects supervisor on major productions): he reports that the head and carcass of Rambaldi's Big Kong are still present at Carolco Studios (which purchased D.E.G.'s assets in the late 1980s after bankruptcy) in the early 1990s. The head, he reports, would be moved from stage to stage while the carcass rotted outside, creating a strange and particularly sad sight. According to Watts, "now [in 1994, ed.] it's a pile of hair and old metal bones... Yet, the first time I saw the monster it gave me the creeps. I felt like I had violated a mortuary." To associate with the sad and final tale about the mechanical Kong we have this photo:

While not wanting to question such qualified testimony, the photo does not seem to represent the mechanical Kong, who became the tireless actor of a film to which he inspired no more than its title.

The Rambaldi Foundation, asked by one of its many fans what the giant's final destination was, replied through Victor Rambaldi (in 2006) that "the creature was probably torn to pieces. We as the Rambaldi Foundation have no idea where it might have ended up...."

But, if this is indeed his head - although we hope that it didn't end up that way at all - did at least the mechanical arms built specifically for some scenes survive?

The two life-size hydraulically operated arms built by Glen Robinson and his team did not survive long after production of the 1976 film. Indeed, by the time of the sequel (1986) their mechanical skeletons were rotting away; therefore, a new cable-operated forearm was created by Rambaldi's team. And that is the one then also exhibited in more recent times.

In short, nothing at all of poor Big Kong seems to have been saved. But that body was not alone.

The other Kong

The Kong of the last scene

Before the Shea Stadium scene, where the mechanical Big Kong is seen for the first (and only) time in the film, another is filmed in which Kong is present in all his static majesty. It is one of the last scenes in the film, exactly the one in which he plummets from the World Trade Center Towers in New York City. And it is a scene actually filmed in late June 1976 right there, in front of those skyscrapers that at the time towered among the tallest and newest in the world (they had been completed only three years earlier, in 1973).

But is it the mechanical Big Kong, later used in August in the presentation scene at Shea Stadium? No. The Kong that everyone remembers, riddled with bullet holes, lying lifeless in front of the Twin Towers, is not the mechanical Big Kong, tossed between the Americas, and then becoming a sad abandoned relic. He is a different Kong.

He is a non-mechanical Styrofoam model, also 40 feet tall and weighing 625 kilograms. And, like the other Kong, he has never actually climbed the Towers (the scene was done in the studio, with Baker in suit and mask). The Styrofoam model, a partly inflatable "body suit," is covered with latex panels covered with Argentine horsehair and is specially made for the film's final scene at the modest cost of $300,000. It is then cut into ten sections and transported on three large moving vans. Once it arrives in New York City, it is reassembled at the foot of the South Tower and surrounded by three hundred square meters of faux terrazzo made of plaster to simulate the surface of the plaza, which likely collapsed as a result of Kong's fall.

Because of the enormous size of the square, Richard Kline recalls that he had to use virtually all the lights and generators available in New York to light it.

Styrofoam body of giant gorilla King Kong lies in the plaza of New York's World Trade Centre in final scene.

Famed urban gorilla dies again

United Press International

NEW YORK — The 40-foot "body" of King Kong lay stretched out on a New York sidewalk Tuesday, ready for the Monster gorilla to "die" all over again.

Hollywood film makers are remaking the 1930s classic movie "King Kong," and the part they are working on here is the end of the picture — Kong falling to his death from a New York skyscraper.

In the original movie, Kong fell from the Empire State Building, then the tallest building in the world. In the remake he falls from the north tower of the World Trade Centre.

But the fall isn't being filmed here — that's being done in miniature in a Hollywood studio. What's being done here is the scene where crowds press around the dead body of the fallen gorilla.

The body, 40 feet of styrofoam, was put in place Monday night and filming was scheduled Tuesday night and today.

Workers spent Tuesday spraying the "corpse" with a vegetable dye that looks like blood.

Prop men touch up King Kong's head, which is covered with horse hair.

Newspaper article on the shooting in New York (1976)

Producer Dino De Laurentiis on the set in New York (1976)

For the scene, as for the one to be shot later in August in Los Angeles, a large crowd is needed, and only a certain number of extras can be paid for by the production... Again, an advertisement is then placed in local newspapers inviting

the public to participate in the shoot. The hope is that enough people will show up to adequately fill the wide shots. On the first night of filming, between 2,000 and 3,000 people show up - a large number, but not enough to fill the square. The crowd is kept behind barriers at the edge of the square until it comes time to get closer to Kong. A first and narrower circle of paid extras is supposed to act as a second barrier to keep the crowd from getting too close, but when action is called the crowd pushes well beyond the paid extras and Jessica Lange, pouncing on Kong and grabbing everything that can be grabbed and carried away as souvenirs. The Styrofoam Kong, in the frenzy of the moment, loses large strands of fur, a fingertip and even an eye the size of a bowling ball. The square is eventually cleared and the evening ends with close-ups of Dwan crying for Kong.

Despite the negative experience, however, the production is disappointed with the turnout and fears that there will not be enough people even the following evening. However, thanks in part to greatly increased local interest following the news circulated in the press, as many as 30,000 people show up. This is a huge number, far greater than expected. Other law enforcement agencies are therefore involved, and numerous extras disguised as soldiers and policemen are even hired to act as deterrents and help control the crowd. Fortunately, when the barriers are removed and the crowd pours onto the square, everyone stops right in front of the ring of paid extras placed to 'protect' the poor Styrofoam Kong. However, Port Authority officials fear that the weight of so many people may even cause the square to collapse, and order the filming to stop.

Thus ends the appearance of Kong's static twin. The Styrofoam ape is disassembled and returned to the production studios. But his working life is just beginning.

Sleeping beauty goes to Paris

De Laurentiis knows how to make investments pay off. And even that $300,000 to make that marvelous Styrofoam and horsehair artifact must play its part, like the other $1,700,000 spent on the animatronic. It has to pay off well beyond the minimum wage object of filming. And so, as with the mechanical Big Kong, the tour begins: the sleeping beauty is shipped to Europe.

For the film's Paris premiere on Thursday, December 16, 1976, *Paris Match*, in collaboration with *Europe 1* and with the sponsorship of *Télé 7 Jours*, decides with De Laurentiis to bring the non-articulated prototype and display it on the Champs Elysées. The 12-meter, 6-ton sleeping beauty is transported, sectioned, by three Super Pelican cargo planes from New York to Roissy Airport. Two American technicians take care of Kong during the trip and its assembly in France: the head alone measures 2.5 meters in diameter, the chest 6 meters and the hands 1.8 meters. And they later tell some French newspapers how they had to clean the giant's chest of the hemoglobin used for the 'blood' effect in the last scene, as well as arrange several specially ruined 'plates' to make the final fall believable (actually, it should be remembered, never happened).

King Kong's arrival at Roissy Airport, Paris

Kong is lying on his back, on the corner of rue Pierre-Charon, opposite number 63 on the Champs-Elysées, home of *Paris Match* magazine.

The well-known periodical then reports, in great detail, on the whole event in its December 1976 issues 1438-1439:

PARIS MATCH
KING KONG
les secrets
de son triomphe
à Paris
Pour la
premiere fois des
ELECTIONS
"SIMULÉES"
Les résultats
de l'opération
Match-Ifop :
L'Assemblée
passe à
l'opposition
Votre
député:
attu ou
réélu ?

KING KONG A PARIS

Sous les fenêtres de Paris-Match

Son coiffeur est venu avec lui

The crowd of people around the giant in fur is such that officers must resuscitate 25 women and collect 33 children who have climbed over barriers to touch Kong. For Parisians, the King Kong scene looks like a riot.

There is also no shortage of photos of the Beast with Beauty, at the time worthily represented by singer Sylvie Vartan:

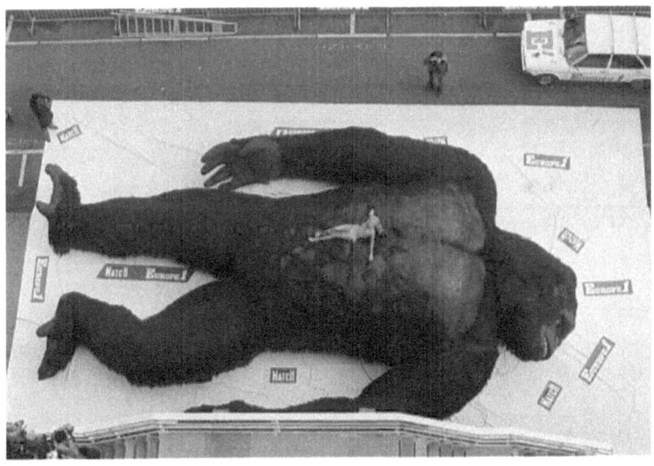

The premiere of the film then takes place in front of several hundred *Télé 7 Jours* readers, drawn by lot.

Having finished his modeling work, the Styrofoam-and-fur Kong goes back to California, locked in a production warehouse near the Los Angeles airport. Always ready to go.

Kong in Ferreri's "Bye Bye Monkey?"

In 1978 *Bye Bye Monkey*, a film by Italian director Marco Ferreri, was released in theaters, winning the Grand Jury Prize at the Cannes Film Festival.

The film is known for a scene (unfortunately 'spoilers' are necessary) in which Kong's corpse appears, lying on the Hudson River in New York City.

In this cinematic work, the King Kong archetype is the subject of a significant reinterpretation by what was one of the "masters of the grotesque" of twentieth-century European cinema. Ferreri's *Bye Bye Monkey* revolves precisely around the dissonant image of Kong's corpse left on the New York coast, next to which Gérard LaFayette (Gérard Depardieu) finds a baby ape to whom he becomes attached (not to be forgotten, too, is the character of the hapless painter Luigi Nocello, played by an unprecedented Mastroianni).

All the scenes in the film, true sketches, seem to want to represent the irretrievability of the relationship between the sexes, the crisis of a solid masculine model and the advance of an aggressive feminine model (it is evident a parody of the feminist world of the 1970s). King Kong's corpse represents, then, the rotting remains of a masculinity that is now decayed and perhaps irretrievable; and the monkey that LaFayette finds near King Kong's corpse seems to open a door for a selfish and one-sided fatherhood, without competing with a female figure.

For the film, shot in 1977, there was and still is talk about the use, for that scene, of the Styrofoam Big Kong, conveniently rented by De Laurentiis to Ferreri's production.

However, there is no trace of this either in the official credits of the film (the set design is by Dante Ferretti, while Bruno Cesari turns out to be the decorator). Moreover, Victor Rambaldi personally confirmed to me that the last work his father made for Marco Ferreri dates back to shortly before his departure for the United States, namely 1975 (and it is, in fact, the film *The Last Woman*, released in 1976). All this, however, cannot exclude the possibility that De Laurentiis, the owner of the film's exploitation rights, was also able to make it pay off in another (and quite different) cinematographic work.

Yet, looking closely at this Kong and the one sent shortly before to Paris, some legitimate doubts advance:

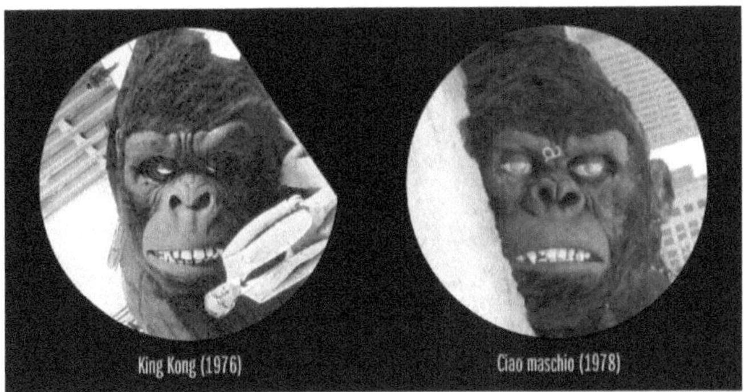

What is certain, however, is the continuation of the tour of the 'official' Paris model: the Sleeping Beauty is in fact leaving for Italy.

Kong in Romagna, Italy

In 1977 an Italian amusement park contacted De Laurentiis and struck a deal to bring Sleeping Beauty (who, after his Parisian efforts, was resting in Los Angeles at the time) to the Bel Paese.

In Italy it arrived exactly on May 31, 1977, on the *Da Noli* freighter of Italia Navigazione, from Los Angeles to Savona, sectioned and enclosed in six containers:

Then, aboard six Gondrand trailer trucks, he arrived in Romagna, specifically in Rimini.

It arrives there because the amusement park Fiabilandia gets the exclusive. To tell us a few more details is Orazio Bizzocchi, who ran the park 1974 to 1987. Interviewed in 2007 by Silvia Forghieri and Roberto Canovi of Parksmania.it, he recalls, "The deal was done then with the old Rizzoli Group, which secured me promotion in its newspapers, *Sorrisi e Canzoni Tv* and others. I negotiated it with the De Laurentis Group, it cost a lot of money but it was enough to communicate that the real King Kong (the movie was released at Christmas) was coming to Rimini and it was done! We had a lot of visitors."

So the Italian adventure begins in Rimini, and in particular in a pavilion of the trade fair association (110 meters long and 33 meters wide) where the different 'pieces' of Kong are placed, as part of the Rimini artisan exhibition "Expo estate '77."

Davide Minghini, *Arrival in Rimini of King Kong*, May 31, 1977

Davide Minghini, *Arrival in Rimini of King Kong*, May 31, 1977

Rebuilt, it is then the subject of a photo shoot (by Davide Minghini) that also features an Italian stunt double for Jessica Lange:

Davide Minghini, *King Kong at the Fair in Rimini*, June 13, 1977

But its final destination is the amusement park Fiabilandia. This is one of Italy's oldest theme parks (along with *Città della Domenica* in Perugia and *Edenlandia* in Naples), officially opened in 1966. Circular in shape, the park is built around a lake, Lake Bernardo, a former gravel pit filled in because of the numerous water tables.

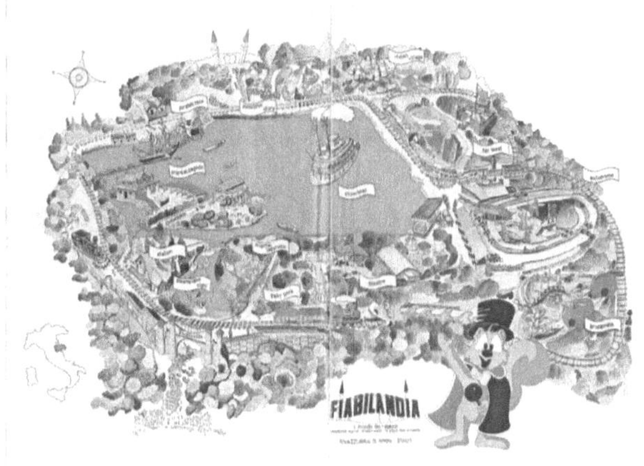

Floor plan of Fiabilandia in 1977

It is not a well-defined park, but it features many forms of entertainment, especially for the youngest children. It is in this burgeoning context that the Big Kong made of Styrofoam and Argentine horsehair becomes the certainly most famous attraction, in the park and beyond: the park gained national reputation, because of the extraordinary guest and publicity and word of mouth, with tourists who cannot fail to visit Kong.

Advertisement of the attraction

Kong is placed, lying down, under a tensile structure. The overall footprint is about 40 by 20 meters. Newspapers, including national ones, follow both the event of the landing and that of the giant's placement in the amusement park:

King Kong
trascorrerà
l'estate a Rimini

RIMINI – King Kong, il gigantesco fantoccio semovente protagonista dell'omonimo film, passerà l'estate a Rimini, dove è giunto a bordo di sei autocarri con rimorchio, che l'hanno accolto allo sbarco del porto di Savona, dove era arrivato dalla California.

King Kong, una macchina del peso di 625 chili, alta 18 metri, è stata costruita dal ferrarese Carlo Rambaldi ed è venuta a costare poco meno di due miliardi di lire.

Rimini (che ha conteso «l'onore» di ospitare il bestione al Brasile e a Disneyland), ha destinato al suo soggiorno un padiglione dell'ente Fiera, lungo 110 metri e largo 33. King Kong rimarrà esposto dal 10 giugno al 21 settembre.

King Kong
a Rimini

Rimini, 29 maggio.
King Kong, il celeberrimo gorilla protagonista dell'omonimo film, passerà l'estate a Rimini, dove è giunto a bordo di sei autocarri con rimorchio che l'hanno accolto allo sbarco del porto di Savona, dov'era arrivato dalla California.

King Kong, una macchina del peso di 625 chili, alta 18 metri, è stato costruito dal ferrarese Carlo Rambaldi ed è venuto a costare poco meno di due miliardi di lire.

Rimini (che ha conteso «l'onore» di ospitare il bestione al Brasile e a Disneyland), ha destinato al suo soggiorno un padiglione dell'ente Fiera, lungo 110 metri e largo 33. King Kong rimarrà esposto dal 10 giugno al 21 settembre.

Corriere della Sera, May 27, 1977, p. 16
and *La Stampa*, May 30, 1977, p. 6

RIMINI — Da alcuni giorni King Kong è a Rimini e vi rimarrà fino a settembre. Noleggiato per tre anni, comincia la sua «tournée» europea dall'Italia e la proseguirà poi sostando in varie città del Vecchio Continente. Per ora il gigante buono di De Laurentiis è in un parco divertimenti, disteso a terra perché non c'era alcun capannone capace di contenerlo ritto: è alto infatti 15 metri, largo quattro e pesa 6250 chili. Due ragazze provvederanno a spolverarlo e a lucidarlo ogni giorno: un lavoro non leggero se si considera la mole dell'enorme bestione di cartapesta.

Corriere della Sera, June 25, 1977, p. 11

King Kong in Fiabilandia, Rimini

Circus Phenomenon

And after that? It is again Orazio Bizzocchi, director of the amusement park Fiabilandia from 1974 to 1987, who provides a clue as to where Kong later went: "I then sold him to Circus Togni, which toured him in Italy and later returned to Fiabilandia. He was then given, threadbare and abandoned, to a traveling show operator, but I no longer followed the latter stage."

Kong's 'life' actually intersects with that of one of the world's most famous circus families. In 1973, the first of the famous Darix's sons, Livio Togni, together with his father started a colossal show. A kind of thrill chest, the "Circus Jumbo," "the most beautiful show in the world," as it is called (and promoted). A production of grand proportions that features numbers that are indeed unbelievable: more than 400 performers and 500 animals. "The biggest production in the world of traveling shows", it is called as such thanks to the performances of the 12-meter-high tightrope walker who walks on stilts, the famous tiger tamer Thierry, and an indomitable Zavatta duo who does, blindfolded, somersaults on bungee wire. All brought together in a show lasting a full three hours.

But the competition is actually international. In fact, in 1975, in response to the European tour of the Americans Ringly Barnum & Bailey, five European circus organizations, including precisely Livio Togni's, formed a consortium, giving rise to an even more pharaonic project, the "Jumbo Super Circus," with performances scheduled for a year in the associated countries.

It was in the context of this colossal circus that, in the fall of 1977, Kong was precisely hosted in a tent adjacent to the main one.

But on how long Kong lasts as a circus phenomenon, it is unknown. Few data are available and testimonies, left to a few hazy recollections.

After the indefinite circus season, Kong certainly returns to the amusement park Fiabilandia. And he remains there until the early 1990s, when the attraction is permanently dismantled. But it is from this unspecified time that his traces are unfortunately lost.

Thus, the most disparate rumors were started: several accounts still recall him attracting visitors to another amusement park, that of Ditellandia in Mondragone (Caserta) in the 1993/1994 season; and then, again, sold to a restaurant in Cingoli, in the Marche region (but there is really no evidence on this destination).

A mystery with no clues and no perpetrators.

Conclusions

"Giant ape, frightening in appearance but human in feelings": this is how the Treccani Encyclopedia defines King Kong under the entry of the same name. But even before the Treccani, King Kong entered the collective imagination, already with the unforgettable, extraordinary 1933 film.

An image that has been punctually renewed, from generation to generation, first with the 1976 remake and then with the 2005 remake.

Still, the allure of being able to see, or even believe you are seeing, a supposedly giant 'robot' on the big screen has something magical and now permanently lost. Indeed, digital has certainly many merits and advantages, but it has literally erased the incredible magic of the analog and mechanical. Thus, to look at that film and its two giant protagonists, to chase them in their 'life' paths after the film, is perhaps a chasing after what we were and what we thought we were seeing. It is the fascination of the unbelievable, which today with digital we do not undergo because we have no doubts: we know right away that what we see is not real, not tangible. It is pure fiction, extraordinary but different.

The fondness that many, many fans, over the past nearly 50 years, have shown for that giant, wondering how he really was made and where, above all, he ended up, is evidence of an enduring magic. No one, for that matter, has ever wondered what has happened to Peter Jackson's Kong: even the children of that time (2005), long since introduced to digital, enjoyed it knowing full well its nature.

Instead, their fathers - to whom this book undoubtedly winks - still today would like to find that giant in some amusement park. It doesn't matter if his legs are not moving much and his expressions are a bit limited like any old man, as long as he is not torn or worn out by the elements, or abandoned in a landfill like it has also been speculated.

Many things have been tried to be clarified, perhaps succeeding; but the author - just one of those children who saw Kong in Fiabilandia in the early 1980s - has not yet been able to close the circle. Perhaps because he still hopes, as many do, that the end is not known but not sad either.

So this is not a 'goodbye,' because I am sure that after reading these pages, more of those children will be able to help me search for Kong.

Bibliography

Essays and articles

Abruzzese Alberto, *La grande scimmia*, Napoleone, Roma, 1979

Bahrenburg Bruce, *The Creation of Dino De Laurentiis' King Kong*, Star Books, New York, 1976

Cantisani Ludovico, Monstra, *fantasie di fuga e virilità lacere. Fenomenologia di King Kong*, in *Delle cose nascoste*, 27 aprile 2021, consultabile all'indirizzo web:
https://dellecosenascoste.wixsite.com/home/post/monstra-fantasie-di-fuga-e-virilità-lacere-fenomenologia-di-king-kong

Chiesi Roberto, Rossi Marcello, *King Kong: la storia, i film, le foto, il mito*, Gremese, Roma, 2005

Denise Dalla Colletta, *"Chegou a hora de mudar", diz fundador do Playcenter*, consultabile all'indirizzo web:
http://projetocopadomundo2014.blogspot.com/2012/07/chegou-hora-de-mudar-diz-fundador-do.html

Erb Cynthia Marie, *Tracking King Kong: A Hollywood Icon in World Culture*, Wayne State University, Detroit, 2009.

Goldner Orville, Turner George E. (a cura di), *The Making of King Kong: The Story Behind a Film Classic. South Brunswick*, A. S. Barnes, New York, 1975

Gottesman Ronald, Harry Geduld (a cura di), *The Girl in the Hairy Paw: King Kong as Myth, Movie, and Monster*, Avon, New York, 1976

Kezich Tullio, Levantesi Alessandra, *Dino De Laurentiis: la vita e i film*, Feltrinelli, Milano, 2001

Lovelace Delos W., Wallace Edgar, Cooper Merian C., *King Kong*, Grosset & Dunlap, New York, 1976 (trad. it. Longanesi, Milano, 1971)

Morton Ray, *King Kong: The History of a Movie Icon from Fay Wray to Peter Jackson*, Applause Theatre and Cinema Books, New York, 2005

Rambaldi Victor, *Carlo Rambaldi. Una vita straordinaria*, Rubettino, Soveria Mannelli, 2013

Russo Giovanni, *King Kong. La "Grande scimmia" dal cinema al mito e ritorno*, Tunué, 2005

Semple Lorenzo, *The Complete Script of the Dino De Laurentiis Production of King Kong*, Ace Books, 1977

Soto Roland Fernando Jorge, *El diente de Kong*, in *La Razón Histórica. Revista hispanoamericana de Historia de las Ideas*, 2015, pp. 202 ss.

Soto Roland Fernando Jorge, *La verdadera historia de King Kong en Argentina*, 2021

Stymeist David H., *Myth and the Monster Cinema*, in *Anthropologica*, 2009, pp. 395 ss.

Turner George E., Goldner Orville, Price Michael H., *The Making of King Kong*, Pulp Hero Press, 2018

Sites

King Kong (1976)
https://www.facebook.com/KingKong1976

Hunter's King Kong 1976 Archive

https://kong.goatley.com
King Kong - Official Facebook Page
https://www.facebook.com/KingKongOfficial

King Kong - Facebook Fan Page
https://www.facebook.com/KingKongFanPage

Carlo Rambaldi Cultural Foundation
https://www.fondazioneculturalecarlorambaldi.it

edizioni intra

SERIES

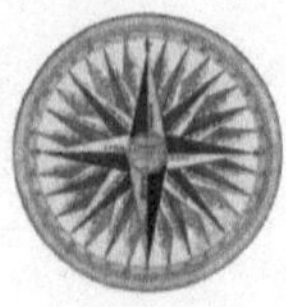

Il Disoriente
Classic fiction
Thriller, Science Fiction, Fantasy

Mysteria
Mystery Stories & Essays

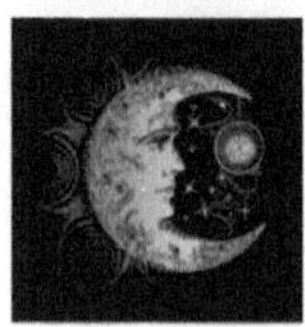

Astra
Stories and tales. Beyond the Earth

Saggiamente
Essays on human and social sciences

Retoricamente
Essays and handbooks on rhetoric,
language and public speaking

Politicamente
Political essays and writings

Brĕvitĕr
Legal handbooks

University

Visio
Graphic and visual arts

Teatro da leggere
Plays

www.intrapublishing.com